# REEL TALK

## MY SECRETS TO CREATING SCROLL-STOPPING SOCIAL

VINCE TORNERO

Copyright © 2025 by Wessler Media

All rights are reserved, and no part of this publication may be reproduced, distributed, or transmitted in any manner, whether through photocopying, recording, or any other electronic or mechanical methods, without the explicit prior written permission of the publisher. This restriction applies to any form or means of reproduction or distribution.

Exceptions to this rule include brief quotations that may be incorporated into critical reviews, as well as certain other noncommercial uses that are allowed by copyright law. Any such usage must adhere to the specified conditions and permissions outlined by the copyright holder.

Book Design by HMDPublishing.com

To my wife and children—thank you for making me feel like I'm the richest man alive.

*"Surely goodness and mercy shall follow me all the days of my life, and I shall dwell in the house of the Lord forever." —Psalm 23:6*

# TABLE OF CONTENTS

| | |
|---|---|
| 01. Let's Keep It Reel: Introduction<br>*(2-5 MINUTES)* | 5 |
| 02. Reel Wins and Why They Worked<br>*(10-20 MINUTES)* | 7 |
| 03. Losses and Why They Reely Flopped<br>*(10-20 MINUTES)* | 22 |
| 04. How I Launched My Own Social Reel Quick<br>*(10-20 MINUTES)* | 32 |
| 05. The Tools I Reely Use<br>*(5-10 MINUTES)* | 43 |
| 06. Reel Quick Pop Quiz<br>*(5-10 MINUTES)* | 47 |
| 07. The Reel Deal: Summary<br>*(2-5 MINUTES)* | 50 |

# 01.
# LET'S KEEP IT REEL: INTRODUCTION

I'm Vince Tornero—president and executive producer at Wessler Media.

I started this company back in 2017 after a career in radio and marketing. Since then, I've helped generate millions of views and likes for clients across the board. I've also built my own personal social media channels from the ground up, racking up well over 10 million views in less than 90 days.

In this course, I'm going to break everything down and show you exactly how I did it with reels and Shorts—and how you can do it too.

But before we dive in, I want to give you a few core principles that have shaped the way I work:

First: There's no "key" to success—it's just hard work. I once asked a high-level exec why certain people made it. His answer? *"They wanted it bad enough."* So ask yourself: *Do you want it bad enough to do the work—over and over again?*

Now, yes—success isn't *just* hard work. It's hard work plus smart adjustments. But at its core, it's still about showing up and grinding it out.

Second: "Business is a process, not an event." That's something a former boss used to say, and it stuck with me. Big wins are great, but long-term success? That comes from having a repeatable process. Processes help you build momentum—and avoid mistakes.

Third: Define what success looks like for *you*. Don't get caught up in someone else's highlight reel. Set your own goals and give yourself plenty of grace in the early stages. You'll learn. You'll adapt. And over time, these principles will become second nature.

Because if you *really* want it—and you're willing to work hard, stay focused, and build solid systems—success isn't just possible. It's inevitable.

---

**Here's The Hook:** Success is about consistently doing hard work, making smart adjustments, and sticking to a repeatable process. Can you clearly define your process in less than six steps? If you can't, why not? If it's more than six, do you really need six? Another way to say "success" is "simplicity."

# 02.
## REEL WINS AND WHY THEY WORKED

Before we dive into the wins, just a heads-up—we'll be looking at some failures in the next section too. I don't want to pretend everything I've done has gone viral—because it hasn't. But I've had enough success to break down a few examples that will definitely help you.

First, a couple of honorable mentions and personal favorites:

- **Deluca's at The Ohio State Fair:** The Deluca's video at The Ohio State Fair came together in a really organic way, with a fun backstory behind it.

    I was originally filming a bit at the Donut Burger stand when the owner of the Italian food booth next door jokingly complained that they weren't getting any attention. I told him I'd come up with something and be back. That moment highlights a key lesson: if you're going to film a bit with someone, they need to be on board and see the value—otherwise, it won't land.

We picked an afternoon when things slowed down enough to focus, because when vendors are busy with customers, the energy just isn't there. Interestingly, the owner preferred to feature his younger employees instead of starring himself, so I had to pivot away from my original concept of him playing a stereotypical, grumpy Italian chef.

He had mentioned yelling at the guys occasionally, so I leaned into that and made it part of the off-camera humor, giving the whole video a frantic, "hastily made" feel. We planned to highlight three dishes, but by the third, the creative momentum started to fizzle. That's when his wife stepped in with a dubbed "mangia!"—which kept things moving, leaned into the Italian theme, and hit the comedic rule of threes: meatballs on a stick, the bread bowl, and the final punchline reveal.

I saved the owner's on-camera appearance for the very end as the payoff. The video ended up with about 40,000 views on Facebook and Instagram combined. When I checked back in with the owner, he joked that he "hated me" because they were slammed selling meatballs and bread bowls. Mission accomplished.

---

**Here's The Hook:** Successful videos need two things: quick buy-in from your subject and flexible production. Get their agreement in about a minute, work in their ideas if they fit, and if you don't nail it in three takes, simplify the plan by removing a step or two.

---

> ### REEL QUICK SKIM
>
> 1. Lead with an intriguing *why* when asking someone to be in your video ("I think you're perfect for this — it's quick and fun.").
> 2. Keep your gear ready and rolling so there's no "set-up pause" to kill the moment.
> 3. Use your phone's selfie cam to show them the frame before you start — it makes people more comfortable.
> 4. For retakes, slightly change a line, prop, or gesture so it doesn't feel repetitive.

- **Buckeye Donuts "Don't Cry":** This one was a lot easier to produce and didn't come with the same kind of backstory as the Italian food stand video—but it ended up pulling in about seven times more views for the client.

  Buckeye Donuts has been a staple across from The Ohio State University since 1969. It's a campus institution on High Street in Columbus, and there's a lot of pride and nostalgia tied to that stretch of town. So when a long-time neighboring business shut down, it sparked a wave of conversation online. I noticed the chatter and started scrolling CapCut for meme templates. Almost immediately, the one with The Rock popped up—and I knew that was it. It fit the High Street energy and sentiment perfectly.

  Instead of using donuts as the background, I swapped in the storefront. That felt right because the focus was on the area, and I thought of the store itself as a kind of "sentient character" in the joke.

The video racked up over 450,000 views and thousands of likes for Buckeye Donuts. A surprising hit for something that took just 20 minutes to think up, create, and post. It was a reminder that keeping an eye on local stories—and knowing when to respond with humor—can really pay off. We've done this kind of thing several times now for the shop with great results.

**Here's The Hook:** Fast, relevant content tied to local trends often beats big productions—especially when humor and timing hit. Follow local influencers, media, and peers, and spend a little time each day scrolling with purpose so you can spot buzz early and turn it into easy wins with memes or quick posts.

## REEL QUICK SKIM

1. Set a 5-minute daily "trend check" timer so it doesn't eat your whole morning.
2. Save trending local Reels or TikToks for quick access later.
3. Have a few (3-6) recognizable backdrops when trends hit.
4. When jumping on a trend, swap one key element (location, prop, wording) so it feels fresh but still rides the wave.

Alright, those were your honorable mentions. We're definitely going to get into my social media failures in the next section. But now, let's get into my top 5 greatest social media successes.

- **#5: Dancing at the Fair:** The first time I saw this idea in the wild was at Disney's Hollywood Studios. I was walking around one night and noticed a random square on the ground outlined in masking tape. Curious, I stepped inside. Instantly, the cast members around me burst into applause. That simple interaction stuck with me. It was playful, unexpected, and strangely magnetic.

Fast forward to the 2024 Fair—I'm working with the "Beach Geeks," a roving band, and that little square came rushing back to mind. I pitched it to the guys: "Anytime someone steps in the square, you play." They were immediately on board. We just needed the right spot and the right moment. It didn't take long.

We set it up off to the side of a busy walkway—not too hidden, but enough space for people to let loose if they wanted. I planted a wireless mic near the band, stationed myself across from them, and we were off. People of all ages jumped in, danced, laughed, and made the moment their own. The highlight? A mom and her toddler dancing together. That was my exclamation point—the perfect closing beat for the edit.

We shot for maybe 15–20 minutes. The final video? Over 450,000 views and more than 9,000 reactions. A total win—fun to watch, good energy, and sneakily an ad for the Fair (which is what social media *should* be).

Here's the real takeaway: Don't be afraid to borrow a great idea. The "dancing in the box" concept wasn't mine—but I made it mine. If something works, remix it.

**Here's The Hook:** Never be afraid to adapt an idea or trend. Make it your own, and let the energy do the work. If something you see catches your attention and entertains you, pay attention to that. Chances are it will entertain your audience, too.

## REEL QUICK SKIM

1. Add one twist to any borrowed idea — new prop, location, or perhaps an audience participation hook.
2. Test the idea fast: shoot 10–20 minutes max so it stays fresh and spontaneous.
3. Position your setup so passersby naturally interact without feeling "on display."
4. Begin and/or end with your edit with the *strongest* reaction moment — the human connection beats the gimmick.

- **#4: Faith and Football:** This one started with a longtime client of mine, The Church Next Door in Columbus, OH.

    If you're from Central Ohio, you already know: Buckeye football isn't just a sport—it's a way of life. And in 2025, that life hit a fever pitch. The Buckeyes went on a title run, and in the middle of it all? Players giving bold shoutouts to Jesus right after the Cotton Bowl. Interviews, press conferences—faith was front and center.

    That's when I saw it. Big moment. Big platform. And they were talking about Jesus? Yeah, this had potential written all over it.

    I started grabbing clips from anywhere I could—pressers, sideline interviews, all of it. I cut it together, added the instrumental from a big Christian track, and set the post to go live on a Sunday afternoon, when folks were back from church and thumbing through their phones.

**At first? Slow start.**

But then I remembered something: Master Teague—former OSU running back—was *on staff* at the church. So I sent him a text. "Hey, want to be a collaborator on this Reel?" He was in. Boom. The thing lit up. 236,000 views and counting. Biggest post the church ever had. But it didn't stop there.

A week later, Ohio State was heading into the National Championship against Notre Dame. And I knew—*if* they won, we could run it back.

**Spoiler: They won.**

We dropped another faith-driven edit and pulled in another 150,000+ views. In total? 380,000 views in two weeks and hundreds of new followers. Not bad for a couple of Sunday afternoon scrolls.

Now, here's the part you don't see: These kinds of posts take *work*. Pulling content from multiple sources, making sure everything's credited, editing it into something tight—it's not a quick job. And on top of that, you've got to move fast. Wait too long, and someone else will beat you to it. Or worse, the moment passes and no one cares.

But when it works? It *really* works.

**Here's The Hook:** Big results come from sharp timing, smart edits, and the right collaborators. Patterns signal a wave—if you spot something 3–4 times in one scroll session, it's starting. Ride it.

### REEL QUICK SKIM

1. Keep a "fast grab" folder for downloading and organizing clips before they disappear. Save links in a notes app.
2. Draft captions and start working on an edit while you're still pulling footage so the post is ready to drop instantly.
3. Use a trending song (maybe an *instrumental* version) under voice clips so it feels current without clashing lyrics vs. dialogue.
4. Tag or DM a relevant collaborator friend *before* posting to lock them in for the launch boost.

- **#3: Fool The Guesser:** We've had plenty of nice wins for the Fair over the years—but this one caught me off guard.

  If you've done content long enough, you know the grind: always needing to post, always needing to produce. It wears on you. Creativity doesn't show up on demand, and honestly, one of the best things I've learned to do is... nothing.

  Seriously—just stop, walk around, and let your brain wander.

  That's exactly what I was doing one hot afternoon at the Ohio State Fair. We'd knocked out the planned posts, and I was just roaming the grounds, letting my mind drift. That's when I saw it.

He was running a "Fool the Guesser" game—silly, quirky, and just the right kind of offbeat. Something about his routine was interesting to me. So I asked if I could film, and for the next 20–30 minutes, I caught a bunch of his best moments—funny guesses, quick one-liners, and the way he interacted with the crowd. It was gold.

I sent the footage off to my editor with a simple idea: cut it tight, layer in some goofy music, and let this guy's personality carry the thing.

And it worked. Really well. The final 60-second clip? 164,000 views on Facebook and 214,000 on Instagram. No gimmicks. No hooks. Just something that felt light, unexpected, and fun.

Sure, part of the reach came from the Fair's strong following—but big audiences don't guarantee big engagement. I've posted things to large pages that completely flopped (more on that later).

Here's what stuck with me: sometimes, the best move as a creator is to… stop. You're your best creative asset, and if you don't protect that mental space—step back, let yourself notice something, feel something—you'll burn out.

If something catches your attention, odds are it'll catch someone else's too. The rest is just shaping it into a story that makes people want to stick around.

---

**Here's The Hook:** Great content isn't always planned—many times it's spotted. Give yourself space to notice ideas, and if something stops you, it can probably stop someone else's scroll too.

---

## REEL QUICK SKIM

1. Schedule "wander time" into your work day— no real set agenda, just observation and thought.
2. When you spot something fun, shoot at least 3 angles (wide, medium, close-up) for edit flexibility.
3. Pair quirky, real-life moments with playful music for instant charm.

- **#2: Glazing Donuts:** Sometimes the simplest post—the one you barely think about—is the one that hits hardest. Here's proof.

It was 7am on a Saturday. I pulled into a diner parking lot, checked my phone, and realized I was about 30 minutes early. With time to kill, I figured I'd knock out a quick post for Buckeye Donuts.

I scrolled through some content and landed on a 7-second video of Jimmy, the owner, glazing donuts. The lighting was great, the angle was interesting, and the glaze shimmered like glass. I typed a caption in our usual offbeat tone: "Saturday morning on the campus of OSU!! We r running hot all morning long 4u." Posted it. Put my phone down. Went in for breakfast. Didn't think twice.

That post? Nearly 1 million views and over 7,000 likes. A follow-up video, same vibe, posted nine months later? Close to 2 million views, 800+ shares.

We've had plenty of successful posts—but these numbers were off the charts. So what happened?

Honestly... sometimes things just hit. You can storyboard, schedule, and strategize like crazy—but the post that goes viral is often the one that took zero effort and felt totally random. I hate that. And I love it.

In this case, it was visually appealing. Raw. Just a good, clean look at something most people never see—hot glaze flowing over fresh donuts. It had that "What am I watching?" quality that makes people stop scrolling.

And truthfully? Buckeye Donuts doesn't run on some airtight, 5-point content plan. We've got a general weekly rhythm, sure. But we didn't assemble a focus group to figure out what works. We just *do it*. It's a reflection of Jimmy—quirky, spontaneous, full of personality. So that's how the brand shows up online.

When I first took over the page, I tried to "clean it up." Fewer emojis. More polish. More structure. That tanked. The audience didn't want curated. They wanted quirky. They wanted authenticity. The weird spellings. The random donut GIFs. That's what felt real.

Look—I'm not saying ignore analytics or pretend the algorithm doesn't exist. But chasing it? Trying to crack it like some fortune teller reading tea leaves? Total waste of time.

Some people try to predict virality. I'd rather build consistency. Nail the vibe. Let the content reflect who you *actually* are. That's the groundwork. That's what pays off long-term.

Because if you're trying to "beat the system" without ever knowing yourself first... you're basically trying to nail Jell-O to a wall.

**Here's The Hook:** Virality is unpredictable—consistency and authenticity win in the long run. Don't compromise who you are for a quick hit. Can you define your style in 3-6 words? Keep your tone and style steady—it can take up to three months to lock them in.

## REEL QUICK SKIM

1. Capture simple, visually satisfying moments that feel "raw" and authentic.
2. Don't over-edit or polish; let personality and spontaneity shine through.
3. Track your posting rhythm consistently—stick to a schedule but stay flexible.
4. Focus on consistency and genuine connection instead of virality.
5. Test short clips (5–10 seconds) showing a single satisfying action.

- **#1: Baby Blowout:** Before we get into my biggest social media success of all time, a quick heads-up: this one's a little graphic. You've been warned.

    So, one evening, my wife and I were enjoying some family downtime. She had our infant daughter strapped to her in a baby carrier, bouncing gently, and I was in the kitchen making dinner. Suddenly, I heard it—a faint splat—followed by my wife gasping.

    I turned around... and there it was.

    The biggest baby blowout I've ever seen in my life. I'm talking full-body yellow mustard-style chaos—on the floor, the carpet, my wife, and, of course, our sweet baby girl. How something like that came out of two tiny cheeks still blows my mind.

Now, my first instinct was to jump in and help. But then I remembered—I had just launched my personal social channels. And here I was, standing in the middle of a parenting moment real, gross, and relatable.

Melina jumped into action, cleaning up our daughter while I paused dinner and did damage control. Miraculously, we kept our two toddlers out of the mess. As I cleaned and filmed, I knew the video needed to move. It had to have a clear arc: the disaster, the clean-up, the resolution. I wanted people to think, "Okay, where is this going?"

A few days later, I spent about 30–45 minutes editing the video in CapCut. I added captions, skipped music (felt more like a vlog), and posted it to Instagram, and my newly-formed TikTok and YouTube.

At first, TikTok had the edge—about 150K to 200K views. Instagram wasn't far behind. YouTube? Barely had a pulse.

Then—boom. Overnight, the YouTube Short took off. Half a million, then a million... then two, three, five. I thought, "No way is going to continue."

It did. Then YouTube flagged it as "graphic," slapped an 18+ warning on it, and required viewers to be signed in. Meanwhile, TikTok and Instagram? Freely available. Go figure.

All said and done, the video crossed well over 10 million views. I gained thousands of new followers and got a few licensing offers (which I declined—I like to own my content).

**Why did it work?**

Simple. Shock value. It was raw, unexpected, and something people don't see every day. Just like the Buckeye Donuts glaze video—it caught attention because it was visually different. The other factor? I had been posting consistently. That built some momentum. The algorithm had probably taken notice.

Here's the irony: I've poured years into documentary projects, high-production content, carefully crafted media. Some of it got a few thousand views. And what blows up? A diaper disaster.

This is why I say I have a love-hate relationship with social media. The highs are incredible. The lows are frustrating. And believe me—I've had plenty of misses too.

---

**Here's The Hook:** Plan all you want, but the internet loves what's real, messy, and unexpected. Effort sometimes doesn't matter—impact does. If it's gross, cute, or enraging enough to spark a reaction, you've got viral potential. Test it by showing the raw clip to someone—if they react, you might have a hit.

---

## REEL QUICK SKIM

1. Don't be afraid to share imperfect, real-life moments that feel raw and relatable.
2. Capture the full story arc: setup, chaos, and resolution to keep viewers engaged.

3. Edit efficiently—30-45 minutes in a simple app like CapCut can be enough.

# 03.
## LOSSES AND WHY THEY REELY FLOPPED

Before we dive into the posts that tanked, let's talk about how I define "failure" on social media.

The average Instagram account has around 150–200 followers. For accounts that size, you can expect about 300 views per reel, according to Social Insider. So if one of your posts performs way below your usual average—that's what I'd call a failure.

*(Side note: those numbers might surprise you. It's actually easier to find success than most people think.)*

Now, I don't have a big spreadsheet with every post I've ever made. I haven't charted them out or built some master analytics dashboard. And honestly? I wouldn't even recommend that. Tools like TikTok, Instagram, and YouTube already show you the data you need.

That said—you *should* have a gut-level sense of how your content usually performs. That's how you know when something's working… or when it's time to change.

So with that context set, let's take a look at a few of my biggest misses—the posts that didn't land, didn't grow, and didn't do what I hoped they would.

Let's break them down and see what we can learn:

- **#4: Cardboard Fort:** If you've ever shopped at Sam's Club, Costco, or Aldi, you've probably noticed the piles of leftover cardboard boxes stacked near the checkout. Some are small. Some are massive. Some look like they used to house an entire entertainment center.

    One day at Sam's, those boxes caught my eye—and an idea hit me: "What if I built a fort for my kids out of this stuff?"

    A few afternoons, some duct tape, and adding in a few spare basement boxes… the "kiddie condo" was complete. And honestly? It turned out great. My little dudes loved it. Watching them crawl through it, laugh, play—that was the real win.

    But then the cardboard creator made way for the content creator. Inspired by our own frustrating experience house-hunting (plus that viral meme of a Little Tikes house listed for half a million), I thought: "What if I turned this fort into a parody real estate listing?"

    So I wrote a fake tour. Way too much time was spent pitching lines to my wife, revising voice-over scripts, giggling to myself while editing. I was sure this one was gold. I posted it and soon after a realtor friend shared it and loved it. I thought for sure I was moving to Viral City, but instead I moved into 123 Dud Lane.

Final view count? About 600.

The engagement was decent—some likes, a few chuckles in the comments—but by my standards at the time, this one flopped. A creative cul-de-sac. Population: me.

Looking back, I can see what went wrong.

First, the housing market jokes were stale. That meme window had closed. I was late.

Second, no people. No kids playing. Just a cardboard structure. Visually interesting for maybe three seconds... then what?

Third, the hook was weak, and the pacing dragged. It didn't feel like it was going anywhere.

My wife and I have a running joke (that's kind of true): "If I spend too much time on something, it's probably not going to perform well." This was one of those times.

---

**Here's The Hook:** The more you polish content, the more it can quickly lose the raw edge people love. Overthinking kills momentum—not everything needs to be a masterpiece. If post-production begins to drag past 15 minutes, see if you need to simplify it into 3–4 quick beats: intro, payoff, reaction.

---

## REEL QUICK SKIM

1. Keep edits quick and focused—aim for 3–4 clear beats to maintain pacing.
2. Don't over-polish; raw and authentic often beats perfection on social.
3. Include people (maybe kids or reactions) to add life and relatability.
4. Remember, sometimes less is more—focus on energy and story over polish.

- **#3: Mr. Rogers Open Always:** If I had a list of celebrities—living or dead—I could meet, Mr. Rogers would be on it. No question.

    Here's my honest take: you either like him... or you're wrong. Sure, the Land of Make-Believe was a little wack sometimes, but the man was pure kindness. He created a sweet, safe place on TV, and that matters.

    Anywho—back to the social media game.

    One of the things I regularly do for Buckeye Donuts is scroll trending templates on CapCut. I'll usually spot a meme or two that makes me pause, and then I ask the key question: Can I make this fit the client's vibe?

    Previously, we had success with a Mr. Rogers meme—the classic "I'm proud of you" clip. So when I came across a newer version, I figured we were in for another win.

    Now, Buckeye Donuts is open 24 hours. Their whole branding line is "Open always, closed never." We use it all the time—it's practically a running gag. Someone asks the hours? Cue the meme.

This post had everything: a beloved cultural figure, proven meme style and was a joke that was already baked into the brand. So I posted it, sat back, and waited.

The result? 5,000 views and 147 likes. Now by most standards—and based on their follower count at the time—that's actually a solid post. Probably 3x better than average.

But by our standards? It flopped. Why? A few things:

First, we probably posted it too soon after the original Mr. Rogers meme that did well. It wasn't the exact same joke, but it was similar enough in tone and format that it didn't feel fresh.

Second, timing matters. This went up around Easter. People's scrolling habits shift around holidays—less screen time, more travel, more family.

Third, and this is just a hunch—maybe the tone came off a little smug. Like, "Seriously? You don't know our hours?" That's not the tone we meant to give, but social media is all about perception, and tone can miss the mark in subtle ways.

The good news? It didn't take long to make. It was a low-effort experiment—and sometimes you need those to learn what not to do. In fact, we're probably spending more time talking about this post right now than most people spent watching it.

So... let's call this one a cheap L—and move on to the next one.

**Here's The Hook:** Low-effort experiments like memes or trends quickly show you what to fix or drop. Break down a flop into three key reasons it failed—clarity here makes your next attempt stronger. But, don't think about it too long.

### REEL QUICK SKIM

1. Test memes and trends with small, low-effort posts to learn quickly.
2. Analyze flops by identifying 2-3 clear reasons they didn't connect.
3. Watch timing carefully—avoid posting similar content too close together.

- **#2: Suave Kazual:** Back in the mid-90s, Barry White did a few comedy bits on Late Night with David Letterman. With that smooth-as-silk, deep-bass voice, he'd deliver lines for "Top 10 Words That Sound Romantic When Spoken by Barry White." It was gold. (Seriously—go look it up on YouTube.)

Flash forward to today: there's an a cappella group called Kazual—spelled that way on purpose—that performs each year at the Ohio State Fair. It's a group of brothers and a cousin. To quote Bruno Mars, they're "smoother than a fresh jar of Skippy."

So, knowing the Barry White skit and how naturally suave these guys are, I pitched them an idea: "Top 5 Things That Sound Suave When Sung by Kazual." Simple. They'd sing super relatable Fair experiences in their signature ultra-cool style. Stuff like, "Hey baby… how 'bout an airbrush shirt?" The concept felt like it was all there.

Production was a blast. We ducked into their trailer behind the stage, ran lines, and workshopped the jokes. The energy was great, the guys were all-in, and the vibe felt spot on. They nailed the delivery.

Then came editing. We added a flashy intro slide, tightened the pacing, layered in b-roll of the airbrush stands and fried food they were referencing—polished the whole thing into what I was convinced was pure comedic gold.

But when it went live? Meh. Less than 4,000 views on Instagram. Around 8,000 on Facebook. Just… meh. Even when Kazual shared it on their own page, it got a lukewarm reaction.

Looking back, here's what went wrong: the hook took too long. We opened with an intro slide explaining the concept—thinking that would help. But in short-form content, the longer the setup, the higher the risk you'll lose people. You have maybe three seconds to earn attention, and we spent those explaining instead of entertaining.

And because I was trying to mirror Letterman's "Top 10" style, I ended up slowing the pace even more—presenting the line before they delivered it. Totally redundant. If we'd cut the setups and just let the guys sing straight through, the video would've moved twice as fast and hit harder.

This wasn't on Kazual at all—they killed it. This one's on me.

Here's the lesson learned. When it comes to reels, Shorts, and TikToks, the hook is everything. If your first few seconds aren't dynamic—or at least feel like they're leading to something — you've probably already lost the viewer. Get to the moment. Make it move. Then let the caption or comments do the extra explaining if needed.

If your best stuff comes at the 20-second mark... chances are, no one will be around to see it.

---

**Here's The Hook:** If the hook misses, the video fails. The first three seconds are everything—grab attention with movement (a turn and surprised look, picking up your phone, doing a task while talking) and punchy cues like *"I need to tell you something," "Here are three most important things about...,"* or *"This might get me some hate, but..."*

---

### REEL QUICK SKIM

1. Start videos with a visual action or unexpected movement to hook viewers immediately.
2. Avoid long intro slides or explanations—jump straight into the content.
3. Cut setups that slow down pacing; let the main content speak for itself.

- **#1: Phone App:** Failures in content creation can be just as valuable as the wins. The difference? One feels great—and the other doesn't.

There's a quote from *The Social Network* movie that nails it: "The internet's not written in pencil... it's written in ink." That's true—if you post something dumb, it *can* live forever. But in today's sea of endless reels, posts, and shorts, it can also be forgotten just as quickly. So really, social media is both expensive *and* cheap. Thankfully, this next one falls into the "cheap failure" category.

One of the biggest mistakes brands—and especially churches—make is treating social media like a bulletin board. Just announcement after announcement. Event graphics. Promo videos. That kind of content kills engagement.

The goal of your social media should be to give your brand a personality. Think of your brand as a person. How would they act online? What would they share? How would they connect?

For churches, constantly posting sermon clips and event graphics without mixing in real personality? That's a fast track to losing momentum. And in this next example... I slipped into that trap myself.

I wanted to promote my client's podcast, *A Year In The Bible*. It's hosted in their church app. But instead of doing a basic promo post, I tried something more creative. The bit was this: I wash my hands, water splashes onto my phone, and—magically—the app downloads and the podcast starts playing. It's a trend that's been done a few times before, and I thought my version had solid pacing and a clean edit.

But... it bombed. Only 400 views. That's about one-sixth of what our people-focused posts usually get.

Here's where it fell short: First, there were no people. Just a hand, a phone, and water. Viewers connect with *faces*, not fingers. Second, it took too long to get to the point. In short-form content, seconds matter. We didn't hook fast enough. Finally, it felt like an ad. If your content screams "promotion," expect most people to scroll right past it.

So, what did we get? A flop. Was it the worst thing ever? No. A few hundred people enjoyed it. It was creative. It served its purpose. But based on our average performance and engagement goals—it missed the mark.

But, with those "failures" comes experience to build success. That's what I did with my own personal social accounts. Let's discuss that in the next section.

**Here's The Hook:** Good ideas fall flat without people, pacing, and subtlety. If you're always selling instead of connecting, you're losing. Skip the hard sell—work your promo into the background, like wearing a shirt, hat, or sunglasses with your logo, so it feels natural, not forced.

## REEL QUICK SKIM

1. Include real people or faces to build connection—avoid faceless or overly abstract shots.
2. Use natural settings or casual moments where your brand or product appears organically.
3. Prioritize storytelling or emotion over hard selling for better reach and retention.

# 04.
# HOW I LAUNCHED MY OWN SOCIAL REEL QUICK

In less than 90 days, I grew my personal social media accounts from zero followers to over 10 million views. It happened fast—and honestly, it was wild.

In this next section, I'm going to walk you through exactly what I did, step by step, and how some of those strategies can work for you too. But before we get specific, I want to lay an important foundation.

Following a recipe doesn't guarantee your dish will look like Martha Stewart's. And the same goes for content. Doing exactly what someone else did doesn't always get you the same results.

This course isn't about copy-and-paste tactics. It's about principles—guiding ideas that work consistently, but only when adapted to your voice, your audience, and your context. Because just like with a recipe, the magic happens in the personal touches.

There's a quote from Conan O'Brien's 2011 commencement speech that's stuck with me: "It is our failure to become our perceived ideal that ultimately defines us and makes us unique… If you handle it right, your perceived failure can become a catalyst for profound reinvention."

That hits. Especially in the content world. So here's a question: Who inspires you? What would be in the middle of your creative Venn diagram—the place where your influences overlap? Knowing that gives you creative direction. Not because you want to copy those people or brands, but because it helps shape your identity and your content with purpose. People don't connect with perfect. They connect with authentic.

Now, if you've been creating for a while and your account feels stuck, that's okay too. You might feel the urge to pivot completely—and sometimes that's the right call. But don't abandon who you are. Instead, redirect. Keep your content grounded in themes and tone that are still *you*, even if the execution evolves. So, maybe I'll take a small liberty with Conan's quote: If your content isn't resonating, let it be the catalyst for effective redirection, not total reinvention.

Here's the big takeaway as you start—or restart—your social journey: Build a framework around your creative identity. Know where you're headed. And if it stops working, course correct. But do it intentionally. Repeat that process as many times as you need.

Oh, and also—watch some Conan O'Brien. He'll *learn* you a thing or two.

Alright, here is how I exploded my own social media from scratch.

At first, I launched my personal social media with a pretty direct goal: promote my business, Wessler Media. I planned to post about current projects, gear, production tips—things tied to my work. And those early video reels? They did okay. Solid start. Definitely not a bad approach.

But over time, I found myself drifting toward more of a *"goofy dad"* vibe. I'd be in Walmart or a thrift store with my kids, filming quick, silly bits—just light, observational humor. It was fun. It fit into my life. And most importantly, it was sustainable.

That shift started gaining traction—and it was solidified when I posted the now-infamous diaper blowout video of my daughter. That's when things really took off.

Now, a few important points for this early stage of growth for me:

**First:** Focus on one platform for your first 30 days. For me, that was Instagram. It's the platform I was most familiar with, so it made sense. Once I got comfortable and consistent there, I expanded into YouTube Shorts and TikTok. That's the key: grow only when you can sustain the growth. If you're struggling to keep up with one platform, adding two more isn't going to fix it—it's going to bury you.

Whether you're just starting or trying to reignite your online presence, the advice is the same: Start small. Start where you're comfortable. Build consistency first. Scale later.

**Second:** Don't overthink every post. Most people will spend just a few seconds on your content. Yes, you should have a direction and a bit of strategy—but don't let perfectionism paralyze you. The more time you spend *agonizing*, the less time you'll spend *posting*.

**Third:** Consistency is key—both in your posting style and your posting schedule.

When I started from scratch, I knew I wanted to focus on video reels. And for good reason—video consistently outperforms other content types when it comes to reach and engagement. In fact, according to Sprout Social, Instagram users spend 50% of their time on the platform watching reels, and short-form videos (especially under 15 seconds) drive the most interaction. If your goal is to build or boost your social media presence, video isn't optional. It has to be part of your strategy.

As for my schedule, I aimed to post once a day. I believe social platforms tend to reward consistency and activity. That makes sense, right? These platforms want people using them—and when you post regularly, you're helping them do just that.

Now, if daily posting feels overwhelming, that's okay. Focus on quality over quantity, and build a rhythm you can actually maintain. Post what you can, consistently, with future growth in mind. The goal isn't to burn out—it's to build up.

**Fourth:** Be very careful—especially in the early stages—about doing any overt promotion on your social media accounts.

When people scroll through TikTok or Instagram, they're not looking for ads. They're looking for entertainment, something interesting, something that makes them feel something. A straightforward promotion for your event or product? That's just not compelling content.

Instead, think about how to provide value to your target audience. Then look for creative ways to subtly incorporate your brand—what I call *"whispers"* of your organization.

Here's what I did: Once I realized my personal social accounts were gaining traction, I started wearing hats and shirts that featured creative versions of my company's name. Not a huge Wessler Media logo splashed across my chest—but stylized, eye-catching designs with the name woven in.

One video I posted recently cracked over 300,000 views. And in that video? I was wearing a shirt with a retro 90s-style Wessler Media graphic. That's a few hundred thousand people who *may* have seen the name—without me ever saying it.

I treat this kind of promotion like a billboard: it's there, it's visible, but it's not screaming at you. You could do something similar—a branded mug in the background, a subtle name on your sunglasses, a sticker on your laptop. Anything that makes your presence felt without hijacking the viewer's attention.

But here's the deal—and it's critical: consistency is everything. One decently-viral video with a logo shirt won't get people Googling your company. But consistent posting, consistent visual style, and consistent subtle branding *will* increase recognition over time.

Social media success isn't built on one lucky break—it's built on recognizable, repeated, value-driven content.

**Fifth:** Don't be afraid to go out in left field and try something new. Yes, you should have some sense of your brand or personal identity—but that doesn't mean you can't experiment. Try different types of videos or posts. See what hits. See what flops. That's how you learn.

Remember: social media is both expensive and cheap. It's expensive because, yes, you *can* mess up and get roasted. But it's cheap because if something flops, it disappears into the digital sea. People scroll, yawn, and move on. You're not risking much by trying.

Early on, I tested a bit called the "AI Comedy Club." I'd feed ChatGPT a prompt and have it generate stand-up jokes—then deliver them on camera. The videos did okay, but they didn't take off. Why? The hook wasn't strong enough, and they didn't really fit my goofy-dad vibe.

So I scrapped it and refocused on humor and content that felt more *me*—stuff tied to real-life experiences, parenting chaos, thrift store finds, etc.

I also wonder if platform changes played a role. Around that time, YouTube started putting greater emphasis on human-generated content. In July 2025, they updated their monetization rules to target what they called "AI slop"—mass-produced, low-effort videos that relied heavily on artificial intelligence. Now, videos without real human input—like voiceovers, original editing, or actual value—can lose their ability to earn revenue. The shift is clear: YouTube wants real people telling real stories. So, why wouldn't other platforms want the same?

It's possible that my AI-driven bits didn't resonate as much because they lacked that authentic, human touch—not just in content, but in feel. That's a good reminder that while experimenting is important, *connection* is what really carries content.

That's part of the process: you try, learn, adjust, and move forward—especially when the platforms themselves are changing the rules.

**Sixth:** After about 90 days of consistent posting and effort, you'll start to get a sense of what's working—and what isn't.

That's been true in my case. YouTube Shorts has consistently been my top performer. Then comes TikTok, followed by Instagram reels. But here's where it gets weird: sometimes a video will explode on one platform and completely flop on another. Same content, same edit, same caption—completely different outcome.

It's like planting three of the same seeds in three different gardens. One blooms like crazy, one barely sprouts, and the third just sits there doing nothing. I wish I could look into each platform's algorithmic crystal ball and figure out why—but I can't. And honestly, no one really can. The algorithms are constantly changing, and what works one week might fizzle out the next.

I also post to Facebook and Twitter (or X, I guess), but they barely register a pulse for me. It's like shouting into a canyon and hearing nothing but your own echo back. Still, I post there occasionally—just in case something sticks.

Now here's the part that's both exciting and frustrating: your results might be completely different. What flops for me could go viral for you. What works for you might bomb on my end. Every audience, every platform, every niche has its own weird rhythm.

But you won't discover that rhythm unless you put in the reps. Do the work. You have to show up consistently and give it time. Social media is more like weightlifting than a lottery ticket. Consistency builds momentum. Without it, you're just spinning the reels and hoping for luck.

So—don't be discouraged by early randomness. Watch the patterns. And keep planting. Something will grow.

---

**Here's The Hook:**
1. Pick one platform for the first 30 days. My suggestion? Instagram or TikTok.
2. No post will ever be perfect. Post more, plan less.
3. Consistency is the critical key with posting schedule and style.
4. Avoid overt promotion. Always offer value *(entertain or educate)*.
5. Experiment with content. See what sticks. Try photos, Reels, memes.
6. In 90 days, you'll know where you're headed.
7. Only grow what you can sustain. Generally, I'd suggest setting a goal of posting at least 4 times per week.

Before we move on to the next section, I wanted to share a few bonus videos from the early days of my accounts that surprised me:

**Mountain Dew Cooler:** I picked up a Mountain Dew cooler from a random gas station—and that video ended up being my earliest personal social media success. It performed best on Instagram, and I think it worked for a few key reasons: the editing had rhythm, the energy stayed high, there were little payoffs throughout, and it was something unique. You don't scroll past a Mountain Dew cooler every day, and that gave the video just enough edge to stand out. Sometimes, it's not about going viral—it's about finding your first spark. And this was mine.

**Olive Garden Pool Noodles:** Olive Garden dropped a set of branded pool noodles online, and of course—I bought a few. We spent about 30–45 minutes actively filming with them, and it definitely paid off. The final video was fast-paced, visually interesting, and just different enough to stand out. It was goofy, unexpected, and had that scroll-stopping quality that made people stick around.

**Sitting With Newborn Daughter:** One night, I was mystified by how my newborn daughter *always* knew when I was sitting down. The moment I'd ease into a chair, she'd start fussing. It felt like she had some kind of dad-sitting radar. I figured this was a funny and relatable parenting moment, so I recorded her fussing and laid that audio under quick edits of me repeatedly trying—and failing—to sit down. It was simple, real, and hit the sweet spot between humor and honesty.

**Toddler Potty Training:** Our son had a habit of yelling "poopy come out" every time he finished on the potty—a perfect bit of relatable dad humor. I managed to catch a few of his hilarious lines through the bathroom door. Later, I filmed my own reactions and edited them in, since a video of just a closed door didn't feel strong enough on its own. The result was a fun parenting moment that was real and brought some solid laughs.

**Dad's Flowbee:** My wife had just given our oldest son a haircut, but it needed a little touch-up. So—enter my dad, or "Pop Pop" as the kids call him. He broke out the Flowbee, that classic 90's "As Seen on TV" vacuum-haircut gadget, and I immediately saw the opportunity. People already love my dad, and the retro weirdness of the Flowbee added the perfect dose of humor. The video translated into over 300,000 views and became a solid early win for my personal social media.

**Here's The Hook:**

1. Hit the hook hard. Nail the intro—visually, verbally, or both. Grab attention fast. Do it in under 3 seconds.
2. Get going, keep moving. The video should feel like it's *going somewhere*. Try to move on to the next clip in 3 seconds or less.
3. Keep the visuals changing and interesting. Keep the motion coming. If you're talking, can you change the setting?
4. Make sure there's at least one payoff. Give the viewer something fun. Does the video cause an emotional reaction of some kind?

5. Use captions. This is basically *nonnegotiable*. People scroll with the sound off. This is also essential to get attention with movement on screen.
6. Write an efficient description. Keep it tight. 2-3 sentences should do. Add 9–12 hashtags. Then hit post.

---

But here's an important note—you'll need to adapt these to your style. You can't really hit every single one in every single video. There are plenty of viral videos where the visuals don't change. But, the hook, going somewhere, payoffs, captions, and description are consistently key no matter what type of reels you're producing.

So far, we've looked at what's worked for me—and what hasn't. In the third section, we took a deep dive into how I launched my own successful accounts and built momentum. Coming up next, we'll walk through the equipment and tools I've used to bring all of this to life—simple, effective gear that can help you do the same.

# 05.
## THE TOOLS I REELY USE

If you've made it this far into the course, it's clear—you're serious about launching or reigniting a strong, effective social media presence. We've built a solid foundation together, packed with the principles I've used time and time again to find real success.

Now that you know *how* to make great content, let's talk about *what* you need to make it happen. Because without the right tools, creating quality content is like trying to cook a classy four-course meal... in an Easy-Bake Oven.

Alright—let's get into the gear:

- **Phone:** This one's the most obvious, but let's say it anyway—you're going to need a cell phone. Before anything else, the two most important qualities of a reel are video and audio quality. If you're baking with a bad oven, expect bad results. But if you've got a solid stove—now you're cooking.

    You don't need the newest iPhone or Android. What you *do* need is a reliable device that can shoot in HD. The good news? Most phones already check that box. As long as your phone can capture clear video and crisp audio, you're ready to roll.

- **Editing App:** I've used two main editing apps: Vixer and CapCut. Personally, I think Vixer is a great place to start. It's simple, clean, and easy to navigate—perfect if you're just getting into editing and don't want to feel overwhelmed. But if you're ready to level up, the clear winner in my book is CapCut.

    CapCut has way more features, more flexibility, and more creative control. Yes, there's a bit more of a learning curve, but if you invest the time to figure it out, you'll reap the most reward. It's hands down the tool I rely on the most to make my videos scroll-stopping, polished, and platform-ready.

- **Mic:** Consider picking up a wireless mic for your phone. You won't need it for every single video, but if you're filming in a noisy environment—think crowds, wind, traffic—it's essential. No matter how great your visuals are, a video is almost guaranteed to flop if people can't clearly hear what's going on.

    I'm a big fan of the DJI wireless mic lineup. The DJI Mic 2 Dual is perfect if you're filming two people, and the DJI Mic Mini is great for solo content.

    There are cheaper options out there—but if you go too cheap, expect weaker results. Good audio is a game-changer, and this is one place where the investment pays off.

- **Gimbal**: If you're ready to invest in one more piece of gear beyond an app and a mic, a good gimbal is absolutely worth it. It helps you capture smooth, steady shots—especially when you're on the move.

  I personally like the DJI Osmo Smartphone Stabilizer. (No, I'm not getting paid by DJI—they just make solid, reliable gear.) Most of the time, I shoot by simply holding my phone or propping it up somewhere. But when I'm filming a lot of content in a busy environment—like, say, The Ohio State Fair—having a gimbal makes a huge difference in keeping footage clean and professional.

  Bonus: you can also use it as a tripod for stand-up-style videos or interviews. It's a versatile tool that really upgrades your production quality without a massive price tag.

  **Dropbox:** When I'm shooting a ton of reels at an event, I make sure to save the raw video to "the cloud"—an online folder that keeps everything organized and accessible. My go-to is Dropbox. There are plenty of cloud storage options out there, but I find Dropbox's interface just works best for me and how my brain processes things.

  Having a folder like this makes it super easy for a remote editor (if you use one) to grab the footage and bring the vision to life. Even if you're not working with an editor, backing up your files is still smart—video files can chow up your phone's storage faster than you'd expect.

  One quick heads-up: uploading big video files on cellular data can totally kill your data plan. If you're not on Wi-Fi, consider only sending the select clips you actually want to use instead of dumping the full raw file. It'll save space and time.

---

**Here's The Hook:**
1. CapCut Pro Subscription for $20/month
2. DJI Mic 2 Dual for $349.00
3. DJI Osmo Smartphone Stabilizer for $149.00
4. Dropbox Plus storage for $9.99 (1 user, 1TB)

---

If you're looking to set a budget, I'd recommend aiming for an initial $500-$1,000 investment to get your social media setup off the ground. That should be enough to cover a reliable mic, a quality editing app (free or low-cost), cloud storage, and maybe a gimbal or tripod.

It's not about buying the most expensive gear—it's about getting the right tools to make your content clean, watchable, and scroll-stopping from the start.

# 06.
# REEL QUICK POP QUIZ

I hope you were paying attention—because it's time to break out those No. 2 pencils and sharpen 'em up. Here comes the pop quiz. I've got a quick list of 10 questions to help reinforce the core principles we just covered. Imagine filling in those tiny bubbles on a Scantron sheet while your palms get sweaty and your brain second-guesses everything—that kind of anxiety.

Don't worry though—this quiz is way less stressful and way more useful. It's a great, high-level review. Let's see what stuck.

**What was the piece of advice a former boss told me that's served me well?**

"Business is a process, not an event." It's important to have a generally established content production process.

### If you're shooting with subjects, what are the two building blocks that make a video succeed?

Buy-in from the subject and your production flexibility.

### What content can outperform complex productions?

Content that taps into local culture and online conversations.

### What should you do with a good idea or trend you didn't create?

Never be afraid to adapt an idea or trend. Make it your own. But don't force it.

### What's the most critical part of a short-form video?

If the hook doesn't hit, then your video won't either. *Or, if your hook don't hit, then the algorithm will quit.* Your first three seconds are the most critical.

### When starting or restarting your social media, what's the important first step?

Pick one platform for the first 30 days. Start where you're comfortable and build consistency before scaling.

### Why should you avoid posting, especially early on?

Overt promotion. People don't scroll to see ads—they scroll for entertainment. Always offer value instead of pushing a product.

**What two areas of consistency does social media success depend on?**

Your posting schedule and your posting style.

**What's the #1 editing app you rely on to make your videos platform-ready?**

CapCut—because it offers the most features, flexibility, and creative control.

**What's the actual secret to winning long-term on social media?**

Consistency and authenticity. Those two things are what really win over time.

# 07.
# THE REEL DEAL: SUMMARY

So, now you've got everything, the reel "secrets," tools, the strategies, the behind-the-scenes stories, and the gear list. You've seen what reely worked, what flopped, and how I found my rhythm. But if you walk away remembering just one thing—make it this: true success on social media doesn't come from chasing trends, copying formulas, or pretending to be someone you're not. It comes from doing the work again and again as the real you. That's the facts - for reel.

There's something magnetic about authenticity. When you create and post with honesty, humor, and heart, people notice. And more importantly, they *connect*. Because at the end of the day, people are following your vibe. Your tone. Your stories. Your quirks. That's what sticks. In the end, just be real. *I mean reel.*

And sure, not every post will be successful. You'll have dry spells. You'll post something you knew would hit and then... nothing. That's part of the deal of being a content creator. But if you keep showing up with consistency—if you keep making content that is authentically *you*—you'll find your people. Or more accurately, they'll find you.

Because ultimately? It's not about being perfect. It's about being consistent. And when you're consistently you, your audience will find you. For reel.

What makes someone stop scrolling? Vince Tornero—president of Wessler Media and father of three—shares the real stories, wins, and flops behind short-form video success.

From viral diaper disasters to client campaigns that hit big, Vince shows you how to grab attention in the first three seconds, stay consistent, and build content that feels real, not forced.

Packed with quick tips, tools, and proven strategies, Reel Talk is your playbook for turning everyday moments into viral opportunities.

---

Vince Tornero is the founder of Wessler Media, a family man, Taco Bell enthusiast, and follower of Jesus Christ (not in that order). He helps clients maximize their social media impact and finds joy in asking, "What if?"

## Follow Vince Online
@vincetornero

www.ingramcontent.com/pod-product-compliance
Lightning Source LLC
Chambersburg PA
CBHW041605220426
43661CB00015B/1188